LIVERPOOL HIGH

LIVERPOOL HIGH
AN AERIAL JOURNEY

HALSGROVE

First published in Great Britain in 2007

Copyright © 2007 images Skyworks
Copyright © 2007 text Halsgrove

British Library Cataloguing-in-Publication Data
A CIP record for this title is available from the British Library

ISBN 978 1 84114 682 9

HALSGROVE
Halsgrove House
Ryelands Industrial Estate
Bagley Road, Wellington
Somerset TA21 9PZ
Tel: 01823 653777
Fax: 01823 216796
email: sales@halsgrove.com
website: www.halsgrove.com

Printed and bound by Grafiche Flaminia, Italy

Introduction

Like many of our great cities, Liverpool can boast a long history, with traces of a settlement on the banks of the River Mersey going back to the first century AD. In 1207 King John granted Letters Patent to found the borough, but the town grew slowly with a population of only a few hundred right up until the seventeenth century. Liverpool's fortunes really took off in the eighteenth century when its situation on the western seaboard put it in an ideal position to take advantage of the West Indies slave trade and commerce with North America. By the early 1800s, 40% of the world's trade was passing through Liverpool, and with it a flow of immigrants, particularly from Ireland, that helped establish its colourful reputation as a melting pot of cultures.

The great wealth generated by this power-house of trade was reflected in the grandeur of its imposing architecture: the Port of Liverpool Building and the Royal Liver Building on the Waterfront; St George's Hall and the Walker Art Gallery; and the Albert Dock, the largest group of Grade I Listed buildings in Britain. The twentieth century, astonishingly, saw the construction of two gigantic cathedrals – the largest Anglican cathedral in the world, built in a traditional gothic style, and the circular Roman Catholic Cathedral of modern design and materials. This wealth also spread outwards to adjoining suburbs and countryside to fund the landed lifestyle of many a Liverpool merchant family.

As trade shifted east after the Second World War and Liverpool's traditional industries and docks went into decline from the 1970s, the city's prosperity dwindled, and along with it its population which nearly halved between 1931 and 2001. Despite it all, Liverpool's vibrant culture survived and has to a large degree led to the city's revival in recent years. Inevitably The Beatles figure large in anybody's list of Liverpool associations and in capitalizing on their popularity tourism has become a major growth area. But there are many other aspects to Liverpool's artistic diversity, including a top orchestra and a strong reputation in the visual arts, that helped Liverpool win the coveted 'European Capital of Culture' designation for 2008.

Today Liverpool's economy is again booming, with the Port of Liverpool now handling more container trade with the USA and Canada than anywhere else in Britain. Its long-term icons, like the two football stadiums and Aintree Racecourse, are being added to by new facilities to cater for the growing influx of visitors from around the world. As you now fly over Liverpool, landmarks from its prosperous past are being joined increasingly by features of its current success to make it truly a city of the twenty-first century and of the future.

SKYWORKS

For aerial shots with impact, look no further...

Skyworks is an independent television production company and a stock footage library specialising in top-end High Definition filming from the air. The company has become one of the world's leading HD aerial archives for High Definition video and stills.

Skyworks is creatively led by Richard Mervyn, the world's most experienced aerial cameraman/producer/director. He works with specially trained film pilots, purpose-rigged helicopters and the most advanced aerial camera systems in order to produce footage of the highest quality.

The Skyworks' team is systematically travelling the globe and filming locations in the unique style for which the company has become renowned. Skyworks' archive collection is already geographically broad and thematically diverse. The company's vision is to continue filming until the world has been covered and catalogued for all to see.

On the television side, Skyworks produces a range of factual programmes, varying from series about history, landscape and heritage to observational documentaries and more recently drama-documentary. Skyworks has produced over 100 factual programmes for international broadcasters, including the BBC, Discovery and ITV.

Skyworks is constantly expanding its product base, as the company becomes synonymous with high class aerial imagery – however and wherever it is used.

In the future, everyone in the world will be able to access Skyworks' content, put together in a variety of engaging and informative ways, allowing them to explore the globe from the comfort of their armchair.

www.skyworks.co.uk

The 'life-blood' of Liverpool – the River Mersey. The docks stretch in a long line from the Liverpool Freeport at Seaforth to the heart of the city. The view over Morpeth Dock at Birkenhead.

An historic warship and submarine berthed at Birkenhead emphasise the
long connections between Merseyside and the Royal Navy.
Several warships were built at the Laird shipyards in Birkenhead.

On the opposite bank of the Mersey at East Brunswick Dock is the Royal Navy Headquarters Merseyside, which accommodates the Naval Regional Officer Northern England and HMS *Eaglet,* the R.N. Reserve unit in the north west, among others.

The Albert Dock was designed by Jesse Hartley in 1846, and named after Prince Albert who opened it.
There were five warehouses in the complex, all built of fire-proof brick, stone and iron.

The Albert Dock warehouses had fallen in to complete disuse by the 1970s. They were restored and re-opened in 1988, containing restaurants, shops, TV studios, the Tate Gallery, and others.

The panoply of Liverpool's historic Waterfront with the city sprawling behind.

Perhaps the three most famous buildings in the city: the Royal Liver Building (left),
the Cunard Building (centre) and Port of Liverpool Building (right).

Over the top of a passing ship, a view across the Mersey to the 'Three Graces' of Liverpool's Waterfront.

The *Finaval* sails towards the sea, captured from the Birkenhead bank.

The Liver Birds on the top of the Royal Liver Building. One faces
across the river, the other across the city. Made of copper, they each
stand 18ft (6m) high with a wingspan of 12ft (3m).

The Royal Liver Building was opened in 1911 and is 322 feet high from ground to Liver-Bird top.
It is owned by the Royal Liver Friendly Society.

Princes Dock. Once the busiest dock on the waterfront,
it is being developed for mixed uses including hotels and offices.

Princes Dock used to be the embarkation point for the great transatlantic liners.
It is planned that a new cruise-liner terminal will operate from here.

The Albert Dock is the biggest group of Grade I listed buildings in the country
and is said to be the most popular tourist attraction outside London.

The headquarters of HM Customs and Excise and VAT at Queen's Dock is
known – perhaps unsurprisingly – as the 'VATican'.

Liverpool Metropolitan Cathedral of Christ the King – the Roman Catholic
Cathedral designed by Sir Frederick Gibberd and built from 1962-7.

Liverpool's Anglican Cathedral, begun in 1904, was designed by Sir Giles Gilbert Scott. At one time second only to St Peter's in Rome as the biggest cathedral in the world, it was not finished until 1978.

The traditionally Gothic Anglican Cathedral, built of the local Woolton sandstone faces
across to the strikingly modern Roman Catholic Cathedral, constructed of steel and concrete.

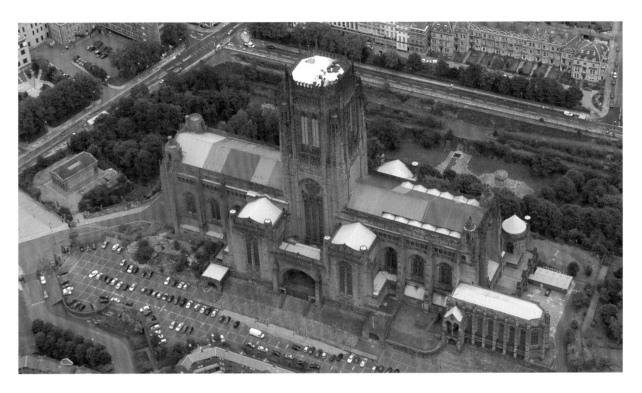

The Central Tower of the Anglican Cathedral, which many regard as its best feature, was substituted for the originally-planned twin towers some years into the building's construction.

The Roman Catholic Cathedral was built on the already-prepared base of a gigantic basilica,
planned by Sir Edwin Lutyens, but never completed. The present cathedral is circular
and rises to a central lantern of steel and stained glass.

The Roman Catholic Cathedral seats 2000, but even this is
sometimes too small and the external altar is used.

St George's Hall, built as Law Courts and a ceremonial hall combined,
to designs by Harvey Lonsdale Elms, was opened in 1854.

St George's Hall was badly damaged in the May Blitz of 1941
and never fully restored until a recent £15m refurbishment.

Stanley Park lies between Liverpool's renowned football grounds,
Everton's Goodison Park and Liverpool's Anfield.

Everton's stadium at Goodison Park. Everton have been present in the
top professional league longer than virtually any other club.

The northern part of the city looking down towards the Waterfront.

A closer view of the city centre from the north east.

Goodison Park. Everton F.C. was formed in 1878 and first played at
Goodison Park – the country's first purpose-built stadium – in 1892.

Anfield. Liverpool have played here since they were founded in 1892.

There are plans to create a new 60,000 all-seater stadium, near Stanley Park in 2010.

Anfield. Liverpool is the most successful team in English football history having won more Football League titles, European Cups, UEFA Cups, League Cups and European Super Cups than any other team.

On the right-hand side of this view down the Mersey is the Waterloo
Dock; it was from here that many emigrated to the New World.

In the left foreground, the East and West Waterloo Docks lead down
to the Princes Half Tide Dock, and then Princes Dock.

The *Royal Daffodil* is one of the ferries run by the Mersey Ferry Company, plying across the river.

The *Royal Daffodil* ferry heading for land. The journeys from Liverpool to Birkenhead and from Liverpool to Wallasey take seven-eight minutes apiece.

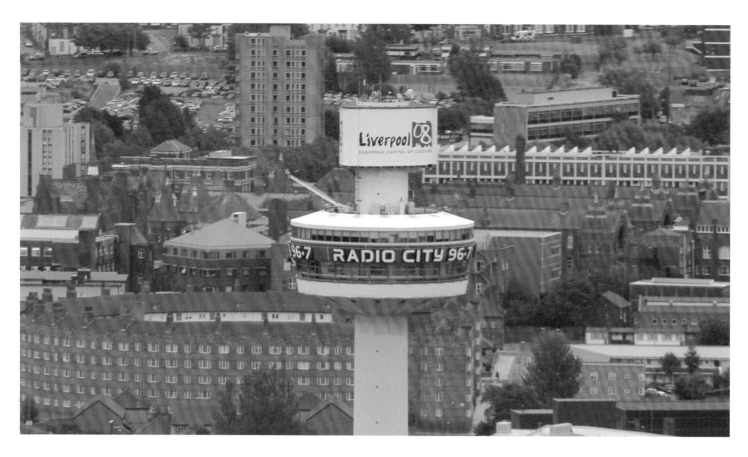

St John's Beacon was built in 1972 and is 450 feet high. Once the chimney for St John's Market, it held a revolving restaurant on the top. This was replaced in 2000 by the studios and offices of the radio station Radio City.

Looking down on the Waterfront. Pier Head, the area in front of the 'Three Graces' is
a popular open space; the Mersey Ferries operate from the landing stage here.

To the right of St George's Hall is the North Western Hotel. Opened in 1871 as
a 330-room hotel attached to Lime Street Station, it was converted to student
accommodation for Liverpool John Moores University in the 1990s.

Canning Dock lies between Albert Dock and Pier Head. Mann Island, the area of land running
up to the Port of Liverpool Building, is the site of the new Museum of Liverpool.

The Mersey Tunnels are administered from the George Dock Building behind the Port of Liverpool Building. Its tall tower is in fact one of the ventilation shafts for the Liverpool-Birkenhead Tunnel.

The roadway behind the 'Three Graces' is named The Goree on the Mersey side and The Strand on the other.

The view over Wallasey, with New Brighton on its right-hand flank.

The mouth of the Mersey with the Seaforth Container Port on the right hand bank.

The view up the Mersey with Liverpool on the left, and Birkenhead on the right.

The estuary of the River Dee with the hills of North Wales rising in the distance.

Looking down over the West Float, East Float, Vittoria Dock and
Wharf and, on the left, the Alfred Dock, Birkenhead.

Meols Parade, Hoylake, on the Wirral peninsula.

The old lighthouse at Hoylake has now been converted to a private house.

The Royal Liverpool Golf Course, Hoylake.

The Marine Lake at West Kirby.

Yachts drawn up beside the lake at West Kirby.

Hilbre Island on the right, with its companions the Middle Eye
and the Little Eye, lying in the mouth of the Dee Estuary.

A closer view of Hilbre Island.

The Caldy Golf Course, lying alongside the River Dee, on the Wirral.

A ship passing the oil terminal at Rock Ferry, Birkenhead.

Over the suburbs of Birkenhead to Liverpool and Lancashire beyond.

Over the town of Bebington on the Wirral.

Port Sunlight. The first Lord Leverhulme founded the Lady Lever Art Gallery in 1922 and dedicated it to the memory of his wife. Now part of the National Museums, Liverpool, it is famous for its collection of eighteenth- and nineteenth- century British paintings and Wedgwood.

William Hesketh Lever, created Viscount Leverhulme in 1922 was a soap magnate who inaugurated a model village for his workforce at Port Sunlight, part of Bebington on the Wirral, in 1888. Named after his most popular brand, Port Sunlight was laid out on 'Garden Suburb' principles with broad tree-lined streets.

Lever used more than thirty architects to produce cottages in pleasing 'Old English',
Flemish and Dutch styles as well as public buildings and a school.

By 1909 there were 700 houses, all occupied by Lever's employees. The rents were fixed
at a reasonable quarter to a fifth of the average weekly wage.

With changing circumstances in the business and different social aspirations, the old methods of managing Port Sunlight had to alter. Over half the stock of houses and flats have been sold and a trust now oversees the village.

Port Sunlight contains 900 Grade II listed buildings and is a Conservation Area.

The centrally-situated Christ Church United Reformed Church Port Sunlight, was founded by William Hesketh as a Congregational Church and opened on 8 June 1904. The architects, as for other parts of the village, were William and Segar Owen of Warrington.

Part of Lever's vision of a content, happy and efficient workforce was that they should
be able to grow their own fruit and vegetables. Allotments in Port Sunlight.

The works in Port Sunlight, at the south end of the village: it was a mere stroll from here to the employees' houses.

Preparing to enter the Manchester Ship Canal at Eastham on the Mersey.

The Manchester Ship Canal was inaugurated by Queen Victoria in May 1894, and was designed to bring deep sea vessels from Liverpool into the centre of Manchester.

The Manchester Ship Canal is 36 miles (58km) long, and is cut from
Eastham on the southern bank of the Mersey to Salford Quays.

Some three thousand ships use the Manchester Ship Canal every year.

The Mersey appears through high cloud on a glorious day.

Looking down river from the Birkenhead shore.

High over the Waterfront. Salthouse Dock behind the Albert Dock is in view, bottom right.
The name derives from the salt warehouses that once lined the quayside.

The Albert Dock, bathed in early morning sunshine. Duke's Dock lies at a right angle to it on the lower right.

Liverpool's rapid growth in the nineteenth century, with a population peaking at
over 850,000 in 1931, saw the building of mass terraced housing.

A sea of roofs – appropriate for a maritime community.

Sandbanks on the Mersey.

Clouds and reflections on the Mersey. The river has one of the largest tidal ranges in the world, sometimes more than 10 metres between high and low water marks.

Speke Hall is one of the most famous half-timbered houses
in the country, and was completed in 1598.

Speke Hall was built by the Norris family and was only sold once – in 1795 – in its 500-year history.

Speke Hall passed to the National Trust in 1943 and is open throughout the year.

The grounds of Speke Hall are an oasis of rural calm, even though Liverpool Airport lies on their very edge.

Liverpool Airport's roots are in the aerodrome constructed in the 1930s on part of the Speke Hall estate at Chapel Farm: the farmhouse became the terminal and the barns the hangars.

Rippling sand banks in the River Mersey.

The Manchester Ship Canal stretches to the horizon at Liverpool. Warrington lies on the right-hand side.

The Thelwall Viaduct carries the M6 over the Manchester Ship Canal near Lymm.

A tanker passes through the Manchester Ship Canal heading east. The maximum length
of ship accepted into the canal is 170.68m with a beam of 21.94m.

One of the seven swing bridges on the Manchester Ship Canal; there is also a swing aqueduct.

The long journey to Manchester stretches ahead up the Manchester Ship Canal.

The towering chimneys of Warrington Power Station.

The Manchester Ship Canal beside the meanders of the Mersey on the outskirts of Runcorn.

The bridges over the Mersey at Runcorn. The channel of the Manchester Ship
Canal hugs the headland around Runcorn on the opposite bank.

The Cheshire landscape opens up on the south bank of the Mersey, seen from above Widnes.

The two cathedrals stand out like beacons in this view over Liverpool looking south west over the Wirral.

The Royal Liver Building has four clock faces: one looks out on the city, whilst the other three face the docks and the Mersey. Each face is over 25ft in diameter, and the minute hands are 14ft long.

Looking down on to Morpeth Wharf and Dock, Birkenhead, with the Egerton Dock at the bottom of the picture.

The broad expanse of Liverpool Bay, looking out over Moreton on the Wirral.

The morning sun on the Royal Liverpool Golf Course beckons golfers on to the links.
The Royal Liverpool was the venue for the British Amateur Championship in 2000.

Rainbow over the Dee Estuary.

One of the figures in Antony Gormley's sculpture *Another Place* on Crosby Beach.

The *Another Place* installation consists of 100 cast iron figures facing out to sea,
and which are spread over 2 miles (3.2km) of Crosby Beach.

Oulton Park Circuit, lies a few miles from Liverpool in the Cheshire countryside.
The British Superbike Championship is one of the highlights of the year.

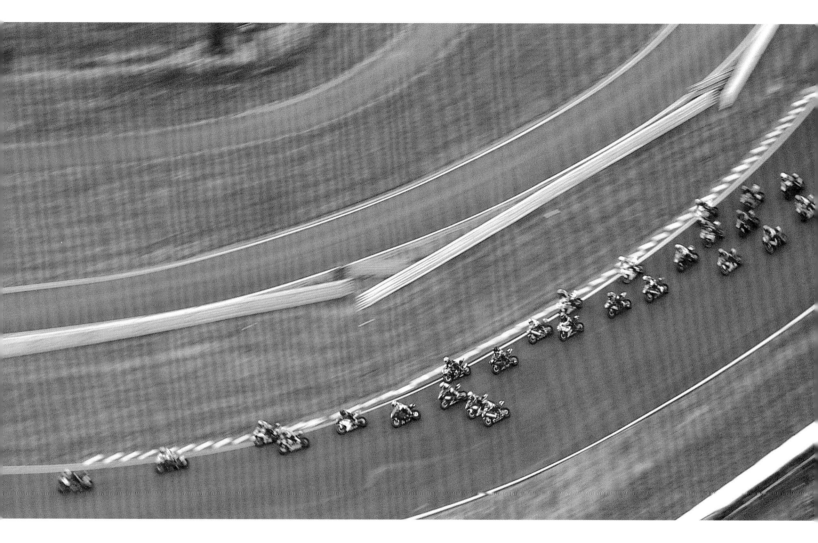

Oulton Park is famous for its challenging corners.

The Island Bend by the lakeside at Oulton Park.

The setting of Oulton Park.

The ICI chemical works at Runcorn seen from Frodsham.
The River Weaver joins the Manchester Ship Canal on the left.

A closer view of the towers, chimneys and vats of the ICI chemical works at Runcorn.
Heavy industry has long been a feature of the Mersey Estuary.

Liverpool John Lennon Airport. Located at Speke in the south east of Liverpool, the airport moved to its present site in 1986 and was re-named in honour of the former Beatle in 2002.

Previously the airport had occupied ground on the other side of Speke Hall,
which is surrounded by trees in the middle of the picture.

Take off!

A wide view of the airport with the Mersey curving around Speke.
The new terminal has recently been trebled in size.

The control tower at the Liverpool John Lennon Airport. The airport is the fastest
growing in Europe, with a throughput of about 5 million passengers per year.

A closer view of Speke Hall and its grounds. The gardens around the house were laid out in the mid 1800s.

The old airport terminal on the west side of Speke Hall is an impressive
example of 1930s Art Deco. It is now occupied by the Marriot Hotel.

Coburg Dock, on the right, and Brunswick Dock together house the
Liverpool Marina. There are berths for 325 boats.

Brunswick Dock, opened in 1832, was another design by the Victorian engineer
Jesse Hartley (1780-1860), who was Liverpool's Dock Engineer for over thirty years.

Lime Street Station, the main terminus for Liverpool. This is
the third station building to stand on the site, opening in 1879.

Aintree, one of the most famous racecourses in the world, lies on the northern outskirts of Liverpool.

The farthest part of the Aintree site, with the Grand National Golf Course, is cut across by
Beecher's Brook from which the famous Grand National jump takes its name.

The first race at Aintree took place in 1829; the first Grand National
in 1839. The National is run over 4 miles 856 yards (7.2km).

Aintree's official capacity is 150,000. The two stands in the middle of the
picture are the Lord Sefton Stand (left) and Earl of Derby Stand (right).

Aintree: the Parade Ring.

Aintree: the Queen Mother Stand (top), County Stand (middle) and Princess Royal Stand (bottom). The winning post is opposite the Queen Mother Stand.

Within the large National Course, there is the smaller Mildmay Course.

The Royal Seaforth Dock of the Seaforth Container Port.

The Seaforth Container Port, looking towards the city. Around half a million containers make their way through Seaforth each year.

Bootle began to grow as a resort for wealthy Liverpudlians in the early 1800s. Some of the large villas which accommodated prosperous Liverpool commuters remain.

A terrace of attractive houses in Bootle.

After the Second World War large social housing developments took place in Bootle.

A P&O Ferry sets out for Liverpool Bay. Ferry services run
regularly from Liverpool to the Isle of Man and Ireland.

Crosby. Mersey Road, crossing the picture from left to right is bisected by the
railway line; Rossett Park football ground lies on the bottom right.

The Crosby Leisure Centre.

Directly overhead the Crosby townscape.

Ince Blundell Hall, just north of Crosby. The Georgian House was built by Robert Blundell around 1720.

Ince Blundell was once remote: now it is sandwiched between Formby
and Crosby, with central Liverpool within striking distance.

Ince Blundell. The pantheon on the right was built as a sculpture gallery. The sculpture was given to the Liverpool Museums when the house became a convent in 1960.

Sand dunes, Formby.

A gas rig off Formby, as this journey ends, appropriately, heading out to sea in Liverpool Bay.